C000000607

BURY ST EDMUNDS

THROUGH TIME

Martyn Taylor

AMBERLEY PUBLISHING

Acknowledgements

This book would not have been possible without the help of several people and organisations, especially the following: Anglia Newspapers Ltd, Bury Past & Present Society, Suffolk Records Office, Rock Bros Trust, St Andrews University Special Collections Department, Brian Coley, Beris Culyer, Nigel Finch, Ann Garnham, Robert Halliday, Bob Pawsey and Michael Smith. To those not mentioned, they know who they are. Thank you. Last but not least, my wife Sandie.

First published 2013

Amberley Publishing
The Hill, Stroud, Gloucestershire, GL5 4EP
www.amberley-books.com

Copyright © Martyn Taylor, 2013

The right of Martyn Taylor to be identified as the
Author of this work has been asserted in accordance with
the Copyrights, Designs and Patents Act 1988.

ISBN 978 1 4456 1769 5 (print)
ISBN 978 1 4456 1787 9 (ebook)

British Library Cataloguing in Publication Data.
A catalogue record for this book is available from the British Library.

Typesetting by Amberley Publishing.
Printed in Great Britain.

Introduction

Trade and commerce has contributed to the market town of Bury St Edmunds' success as the hub of East Anglia. The wool trade in medieval times was an important factor in this. Bury Fair was acknowledged as one of the most important fairs in the country from its early beginnings in the twelfth century until its closure in 1871. Possibly the oldest purposely laid-out town in the country, you can still follow the medieval grid and its fine buildings that one celebrated visitor to the town, Daniel Defoe, once described as 'the Montpellier of England'.

Through the many manuscripts of the once magnificent Benedictine abbey built to glorify the remains of St Edmund, once patron saint of England, we know how life was at the abbey; the chronicle of the monk Joscelin de Brakelond details just such. Unfortunately, we don't know how the other half lived: the townspeople. The odd rebellion here and there against the abbey's controlling influence only gives a glimpse of what life was really like. Gradually the many narratives written by various scholars over the years have enabled us to visualise the past. However, it is the photographic image that we can connect with the most. To the often used phrase, 'a picture paints a thousand words' could be added 'and triggers many memories' when it comes to photographs.

While we have lost many of the iconic shops our descendants took for granted, the town does still have many individual and independent shops, something we are very proud of. However, the asset that can be rightly called the 'jewel in the crown' of Bury St Edmunds is the glorious Abbey Gardens. These gardens, lovingly created before Victoria was even on the throne, contribute so much to tourism in the town and to the many awards that Bury has reaped in its quest to be rightly called Britain's floral town. Situated on much of the old abbey site you can still wander between flowerbeds as our Victorian and Edwardian ancestors did. Unfortunately, black-and-white photographs do not do true justice to the beauty of these flowered delights, although modern coloured pictures certainly do!

As the gardens are tended and cared for, so is the town itself, by the Bury Society. It was created in 1971 by concerned residents in opposition to the wholesale destruction of St Johns Street; a street thankfully still in existence today with an eclectic mix of shops. This civic society, a watchdog of good planning and design, appreciates that just as Bury St Edmunds has to go forward into the twenty-first century it has to care for its past today, for the future.

We are very fortunate in the town to have a wonderful archive of photographic images; there is the Spanton Jarman collection of photographic plates – its custodians are the Bury St Edmunds Past and Present Society. These images and others by local photographers of the late nineteenth and the twentieth century not only give us an insight into life then but unbelievably so many of them could easily be taken now. This is what this book is about, then and now.

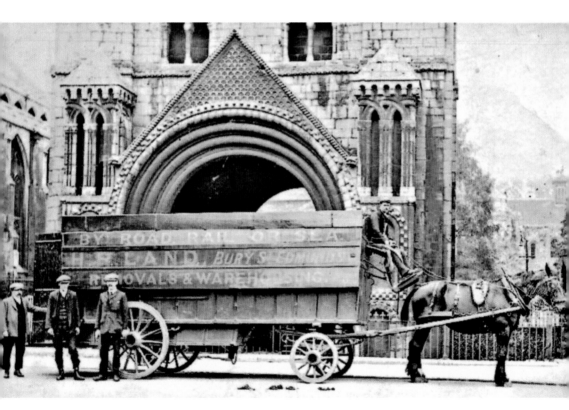

Abbeygate, Angel Hill
In 1327, the townspeople revolted against the oppressive control of the abbey, destroying its secular entrance. In those days the gate stood opposite Abbeygate Street and was known then as The Cook Row. By 1347 this very iconic gateway was finished in the English Decorated style with niches for statues and embellishments. At 60 feet high and with walls up to 6 feet thick, a small garrison was stationed here by leave of the king. A Victorian replacement, the portcullis has never been lowered!

The Dove, Hospital Road

Soon after this pub started out as a Victorian beerhouse, the nearby Thingoe Union workhouse in Mill Road was built by William Steggles in 1836. The Dove finally got its full licence in 1929. For many years Tommy Reach was a popular landlord here. The pub expanded in 1986, adding on the adjacent cottage, but then somehow lost its way. However, it is now back on track, a CAMRA rated proper pub.

Elephant & Castle

Ellen (Ellie) Bruton was local brewer Greene King's longest serving landlady. She worked well into her nineties at what was affectionately known as the 'Trunk' in Hospital Road. Her one-armed husband (railway industrial accident) Joe predeceased her by some years, leaving this matriarchal figure to run a hostelry frequented by local characters such as Les Freeman, 'Ebbler' Green and Jimmy Dodds, legendary drinker. Due to cutbacks the 'Trunk' closed in 2012 and will sadly be missed.

Fox Inn, Eastgate Street

Possibly the oldest public house in the town, the Fox Inn escaped the ravages of the great fire of Bury in 1608, which started further up Eastgate Street in a maltster's. Inside, the roof has many fine timbers including an octagonal crown post. The Victorian exterior makeover of pseudo-Jacobean black-varnished timbers was removed by Greene King in 1922, as were several layers of paint on genuine Jacobean panelling internally. Once a drover's inn, it is now an open-plan gastropub.

Dog & Partridge

Once the Mermaid Inn, this ancient pub in Crown Street was taken over by Greene King in 1872. Landlords applied for midnight extensions whenever a popular performance at the nearby Theatre Royal took place. The theatre's patrons no doubt enjoyed the rook pies, a speciality of the pub, the rooks being shot in the churchyard at nearby St Mary's. Throughout the years many alterations have taken place internally and externally including removal of the mock Jacobean timbers as at the Fox and contentious changes of inn signs!

Golden Lion Brewery, St Andrews Street South

This was one of several independent breweries in the town, with a tap at No. 57 Guildhall Street – both closed in 1907. On the site of this brewery, new owners the Warren family had a forge and there was Barker's fish and chip shop at one end; first Marshams Tyre Co. then National Tyres operated from the other. Much of the site was cleared for housing in 2003, the timber-clad building being retained.

Greene King Brewery Chimney, from Bridewell Lane
Contrary to popular belief, Greene King was formed by the amalgamation of Edward Greene's Westgate Brewery and Fred King's St Edmunds Brewery in 1887. The Victorian brick chimney was demolished in the 1980s, replaced by a triple metal pipe stack. One of these is a dummy, not only to give it stability but a more aesthetic appearance. Now one of the largest independent brewers in the country, Greene King is also one of the town's major employers.

Unitarian Meeting House, Churchgate Street

In 1711 this wonderful Presbyterian chapel was built by Pastor Samuel Bury and his congregation in record time. It is as beautiful internally as it is externally, with original box pews and a triple-decker pulpit; the brickwork is exceptional, old English Bond. Over the years a lot of restoration has taken place including bringing it up to date for modern needs. A newly designed knot garden has recently been created at the front.

All Saints Church

The Parish of All Saints was created in 1953 to serve the Priors estate and surrounding district. The church on the corner of Park Road and Highbury Road, built in 1962 by Harvey Frost, was consecrated in January 1963 by the Bishop of St Edmundsbury and Ipswich. This 20-foot spire, erected in December 1962, had a bell-shaped speaker inside to simulate bells – alas now defunct! In recent years a covered way was built between the church and 1953 church hall.

West Front of the Abbey Church

At 246 feet across this was one of the widest in the country! With octagonal chapels and a tower we can only speculate the height of, this must have presented a magnificent entrance to the Abbey Church. The last great procession to go through its central arch was that of the funeral cortège of French queen Mary Tudor, Henry VIII's sister, in 1533. After the Dissolution, houses were built into the ruined front, thankfully restored in recent years.

Interior of St Mary's

As you look down the nave of St Mary's you appreciate the beauty of this, one of the largest parish churches in England. In this picture, the church is about to celebrate a harvest festival service. The oldest endowed service in the country from 1481 to benefactor Jankyn Smyth is still celebrated here in June. The magnificent hammer beam roof is of a procession of angels leading to the east window of 1844 with the martyrdom of St Edmund in stained glass.

The Dovecote, Abbey Gardens
Also known by the French name of 'Colombier' in medieval days, a dovecote was an important source of food for the monks. Still evident are the nesting holes. Being so close to the River Lark, this area was always prone to flooding. This is what happened in 1879 when a grand gala with all sorts of attractions was wiped out following torrential rain. In modern times the Abbey-Fest near this spot with various live music entertainments has been very popular.

The Abbots Bridge

Spanning the River Lark, this very iconic bridge has open buttresses on one side through which planks could run; this allowed the townspeople to cross the river. On the abbey side, the monks could cross uninhibited, an iron grating being lowered if necessary to prevent any unwanted visitors on the river. The Eastgate, the only town gate controlled by the abbot, was also nearby, handy in times of trouble. The bridge has changed very little in nearly 900 years!

Drinking Fountain, Abbey Gardens

This ornamental drinking fountain stood in the Traverse after the Marquess of Bristol gave it to the town in 1871. It was moved to the Abbey Gardens in 1939 to create space for traffic. Recently, the sundial and inscription on the face of the Portland stone has been found to be of major importance in the world of horology. Calculations on a graph called 'the equation of time' relates to Greenwich Mean Time. Hopefully it will soon be restored.

Churchyard Avenue

This is one of two lime tree avenues in the Great Churchyard. On the right is Samson's Tower, part of the west front of the Abbey Church; it became the Probate Office in later years. On the left is the ivy-covered ruined charnel house from 1301, once a consecrated bone depository. In 1721, a barbarous attack in the churchyard by Arundel Coke on his brother-in-law left him disfigured, resulting in Coke paying the full penalty! Thankfully all is now tranquil.

The Abbots Graves

While researching in Douai, France, M. R. James, famous ghost writer and academic, discovered evidence of the location of five abbot's graves in St Edmundsbury Abbey. They were uncovered here in the Chapter House on New Year's Day 1903. Most famous was that of Abbot Samson, friend of Richard the Lionheart. Local stonemasons Hanchets re-cut new inscriptions (reputably on the undersides of the coffin lids), turning them uppermost for the sum of £8 12s! As far as is known the remains are still here.

Magna Carta Plaques

Just visible among the 1909 undergrowth are two plaques on a column of the Abbey Church's Crossing. Both plaques were put there in the mid-nineteenth century under the auspices of Dr Donaldson, the headmaster of Bury Grammar School. They tell the story of Magna Carta, with a list of the barons who met here in 1214 (according to medieval chronicler, Roger of Wendover). As one of the five towns of the Magna Carta Trust, 2014 sees the 800-year anniversary.

Abbey Precincts

At the beginning of the last century the two properties here were known as 'Abbey Ruins'. The Marquess of Bristol's land agent, Henry Donne, lived at No. 1. He had a large part of the Abbey Church including the Chapter House in his gardens to the rear. In 1903 he paid for the exhumation of five of the abbots that were buried here. The Precincts are now owned by the Diocese of St Edmundsbury and Ipswich.

Gravestones by Cathedral

This part of the churchyard by St James near the abbey's west front was covered in graves up to the late 1950s. The headstones were removed and the graves' occupants left in situ. The cathedral then still had its Victorian chancel and no tower. A sward of grass was laid, then a remarkable bronze statue of St Edmund, created by renowned sculptress Dame Elizabeth Frink, was erected in 1976 to observe the amalgamation of East and West Suffolk in 1974 into the county of Suffolk.

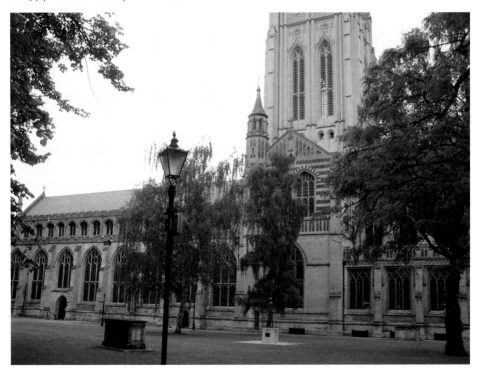

The Cathedral Church Tower of St James & St Edmund

When the architect of St Edmundsbury and Ipswich Diocese, the acrophobic Stephen Dykes Bower, died in 1994, he left over £2 million in his will for the addition of a tower. He had already completed major works here including a new choir and crossing. Former associate Hugh Mathew was able to finish the work when a successful bid to the Millennium Commission enabled the tower to start in 2000. It was finished in 2005 to triumphant acclaim.

The Norman Tower

Abbot Anselm, abbacy 1120–48, built this impressive 80-foot-high gateway to the Abbey Church. Constructed from Barnack limestone it is one of the finest Norman buildings in the country. However, in danger of collapse some 700 years later, restoration was undertaken and included removing properties abutting the tower. Adjacent, Savings Bank, a pseudo-Jacobean house, was built at the same time to designs by tower restoration and Gothic Revival architect Lewis Cottingham. The tower is now the belfry for the cathedral.

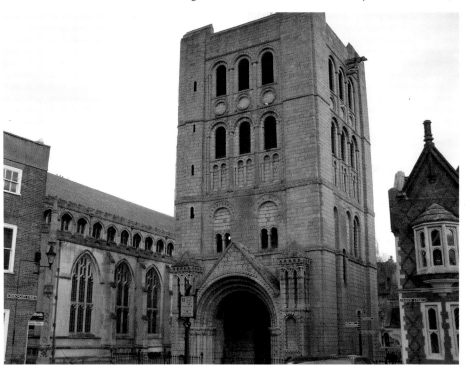

F. Mudd & Son, Church Row

Frank Mudd started off as a coal merchant and dairyman before progressing onto furniture removals. 'It's a pleasure to be of service' and 'Fully insured and experienced packing' were the promissory words on the trading cards of this family firm. Also capable of heavy haulage, it was in business for over sixty years until it was taken over in the mid-1960s. Properties run by Stonham Housing Association were built on the site, appropriately now called Mudds Yard.

H. R. Land Removals

A family firm at Nos. 30–31 Churchgate was started in 1905 by Harry Land. It is mentioned in several directories as in Kellys as 'art house furnishers and removals'. They also retailed soft furnishings, bedding and carpets. Harry's son and daughter ran the business for fifty years from 1929. National removal firm Pickfords then took over but after three more years H. Land ceased trading, closing down in 1982. The shop became firstly Mortimer's fish restaurant then Maison Bleu restaurant.

Borough Cemetery Chapel

This surviving chapel (the other to Nonconformists was demolished several years ago after a disastrous fire) was built to designs by architects Cooper & Peck. The land was purchased by the borough in 1855 from George Brown of Tostock. He gave his name to nearby Upper and Lower Brown Road, which would later become Queens and York Road. The purchase of further land in 1880 increased the size of the cemetery to about 15 acres. Today, internments are reaching full capacity.

ENTRANCE TO CEMETERY, BURY ST. EDMUNDS

Borough Cemetery Entrance

Built for the cemetery caretaker, the lodge at the entrance was constructed of Kentish rag stone, as were the two chapels. It opened for burials in October 1855, the Great Churchyard, closing a year earlier because of government hygiene regulations. The cemetery was approached by a rural lane, Field Lane, which soon changed to Cemetery Road, changing again to Kings Road to celebrate the Coronation of George V in 1911. Mr and Mrs Long, shown here, were the caretakers for many years.

Corn Exchange & Abbeygate Street

One of Bury's major public buildings was built by Lot Jackaman in 1861/62. Mid-twentieth-century wrestling and roller skating was held here. Saved from demolition in 1959/60 and 1970 it was split in two, with shops below and a public hall above. Opposite were the Alliance Assurance offices, now Café Rouge. Walkers Stores, grocer's, are in the foreground, their broken biscuits a child's cheap treat! National pub chain J. D. Wetherspoon controversially leased the public venue, with the Corn Exchange pub opening on 5 June 2012.

Abbeygate Street

In medieval times this was known as The Cook Row, becoming Abbeygate Street in 1792. Around this time, many of the shopfronts, no better than open stalls, were enclosed. On the left, Greggs, a triple-gabled building with its original Georgian windows, started out as Oliver's the grocer's. Opposite is Shoephoric, once Quants, shoemakers from the nineteenth century. Thurlow Champness, jeweller's, is on the left, one of the town's oldest businesses. Looking down, an open countryside view from Abbeygate Street is now protected.

Provision Market, Cornhill

The second building on the right was a corn exchange in 1836. Eventually found to be too small, it was decided to build a larger exchange nearby in 1861. The old exchange became an enclosed provisions market; however, it was short lived due to opposition by traders. Over time it became the School of Art, Borough Library, public conveniences and even at one end a fire station! Today it is still multifunctional but with a tea room and shops.

St Edmunds Fayre

This short-lived shopping mall on The Cornhill was built on the site of a Sainsbury's supermarket. Costing over £2 million, it had a first-floor restaurant called the Blue Note along with a mix of thirteen shops. Despite the novelty of having your meal accompanied by a jazz piano, the Blue Note closed and so did the shops, the ill-fated Fayre finishing in 1993. The mall was completely reconfigured and went back to its origins as another supermarket, Iceland.

Corn Hill,
Bury St. Edmunds.

Cornhill Looking East

From medieval times this part of the Beast Market was also known as Hogs Hill. In 1828, the Beast Market moved to St Andrews Street South. Moyses Hall, the Borough Museum since 1899, is on the left. Once thought to be a synagogue, its location debunks this theory; it survived Bury's great fire of 1608. The Linens Direct, Starbucks and Thomas Cook buildings are post-fire; at the latter the Bullen family had their cabinetmaking and removals premises, 1855–1920s.

Cornhill Looking West

Apart from the post office from 1895, there has been a lot of change in this area. Gone are grocers Lipton's and Maypole, as has that stalwart of the high street F. W. Woolworth Co.; their bazaar came to Bury in 1929, replacing draper Charles Best. 'Woolies' then moved into larger premises in 1952. The promised link to the Arc shopping development using Market Thoroughfare, alongside the post office, never did materialise! The market is still held twice weekly.

King Edward VI Grammar School, The Vinefields
One of the oldest grammar schools in the country from 1550, the grammar school moved here in 1883 from Northgate Street. Previously it had been in Eastgate Street. Local pupils were known as Royalists and others as Foreigners. When the KEGs, as it became colloquially known, moved in 1972 to Grove Road because of the comprehensive system, this building became part of St James Middle School. In recent years it became apartments, although St James continues to flourish nearby.

Guildhall Feoffment School

The Commercial School in College Street was established, as was its elementary counterpart in Bridewell Lane, by the Guildhall Feoffees (founded in medieval times by Jankyn Smyth). As the Commercial School it was to teach 158 boys not only 'the three Rs' but French, Latin, surveying, etc., in preparation for professional careers. Henry Kendall designed the school in 1843. Both schools amalgamated in 1931, somewhat enlarged since then. The stepped parapet with the armorial shields, one to Jankyn, has now gone.

Moreton Hall

This large house on the eastern side of the town was built in 1773 for John Symonds, professor in Modern History at Cambridge University. It was known then as St Edmunds Hill. One of its notable features is the drawing room designed by Robert Adam. Today it is Moreton Hall Preparatory School, lending its name to a nearby urban sprawl of modern housing and commercial properties that began in the 1970s and is known today as the Moreton Hall estate.

Pageant of 1907

The Town Improvement Committee, who organised this historic celebration of Bury, including the life and death of St Edmund, employed a pageant master, Louis Napoleon Parker, responsible for two other pageants. It was played out in and around the Abbey Gardens, a most suitable backdrop. These characters are King Henry I and second wife Adela from episode III played by Mr and Mrs Reginald Bascombe. Bury printers Pawseys produced sets of tinted pageant postcards. Below, the author is with Harvey the labradoodle – not quite a horse!

Langton Garage

When this garage was owned by the Todd family, it offered safe undercover parking. During demolition to make way for Langton Place, a shopping thoroughfare linking Whiting Street and Hatter Street, a limestone fireplace was found in situ – a possible vestige of when it was known as Heathenmens Street, the medieval Jewish quarter of Bury. Archbishop Stephen Langton of Canterbury helped the barons organise the Magna Carta after their meeting at St Edmundsbury Abbey in 1214. Huwrays Autos subsequently became a restaurant, and is now a newsagent.

Cinema Garage

The Central Cinema in Hatter Street opened in 1924, and underwent many name changes over the years; currently it is the Abbeygate Picturehouse. When 'Duggie' Holden, who had run his aptly named Central Garage at the rear in Angel Lane for many years, finished, Sid Lawrence and Russell Mansfield took over, renaming it Cinema Garage. Peter Unwin later took over from Sid. This was in business for several years until it closed around 1996. Housing is now on the site.

Rogers Garage, Whiting Street

Barehams offered a full taxi service from their 'Ideal Garage'. Later, Fairtax Travel of Brentgovel Street also had a garage here. Brothers Pat and Neville Rogers started theirs in 1979 – Pat's ramp is on the right and Neville's on the left. In 1997 it was the last town centre garage to dispense fuel. Sadly, after Neville died, the garage closed in 2010. Patrick House on the right and Neville House on the left are the new houses – a nice touch by the developers!

C. J. Bowers & Son

Charles and George's motorcycle business started at No. 98a Risbygate Street, a former stable in 1928. It soon expanded, taking over a private house and Barlow's commercial hotel at No. 100, which had just closed. An increase in sales led to further expansion by George's son, Brian, in 1988, when they moved over the road to Nos. 11 and 13, where the Chevron fuel station used to be. This year, 2013, sees this family orientated business celebrate twenty-five years here.

Lawson's

Cyril Lawson is credited with bringing television to Bury St Edmunds in the 1930s. His shop on the site of the former Empire cinema (destroyed by fire in 1926), on the corner of Market Thoroughfare and St Andrews Street South, sold electrical goods. Cyril, a motorcycle enthusiast, also expanded into vehicle maintenance on his firm's vans, thus creating his own garage. Lawson's closed in 1999, and the buildings are now a nail bar and bookmaker's. Some staff started afresh and formed Newlife TV in Garland Street.

W. Herrington

Just after the First World War, Walter Herrington purchased a grocer's shop here at No. 26 Risbygate Street. His son Joe with his wife Jean expanded it, newspaper deliveries and knitting wool their staple business. After fifty years of trading, getting up early to see off the delivery boys and girls, it was time to call it a day and they retired in 1998. The shop was sold to become a private residence and any trace of its former existence was completely eradicated.

D. Berry

Since the reign of George III a bakery had been on the premises of No. 34 Churchgate Street. Proof of this is an embossed oven plate in situ with the King's name on. F. Woolnough ran it as a baker's and confectioner's till Dansie Berry purchased it in 1905. Stanley Pugh took it over as a going concern in 1954. Stan died in 1994. Paddy, Stan's son, had his last bake five years later. It is now a private house.

Finches Bakery

There had been a bakery here in Out Westgate for over a hundred years. At the rear of the building behind the ovens, the interior was cut deep into the chalk. The bakery was owned by the Chinery family before Walter Finch took over in 1934. Son Nigel is pictured here not long before the West End Bakery closed on 4 May 2004, finally relinquishing family ties. Part of it in 2013 is a tattoo studio.

Baxters

Samuel Baxter, cutler, was trading during the mid-nineteenth century at No. 91 St Johns Street. A 1939 advert called it 'the noted house for high class cutlery'. Mr and Mrs Barnard were the proprietors of this very quaint shop for many years. It also sold fancy goods and was probably the last place in town you could get your knives and scissors sharpened! Their business closed in 1991. Today it is the Bury Sewing & Knitting shop.

Andys Records

Andy Gray started selling cut-price records and cassettes from market stalls in Cambridge and Bury in 1974. From these humble beginnings he had twenty-six stores by 1995, including this St Johns Street branch. The same year Andys Records won the best independent record retailer award in the UK again. Facing fierce competition from HMV and Virgin he sadly went into administration in May 2003. Jaegar, an upmarket clothing chain originally founded in 1884 by Lewis Tomalin, is now based here.

Debenhams, Buttermarket
When E. W. Prettys department store closed on this site around 1978, Debenhams moved in, albeit for twenty years. They also had a homeware branch in the Traverse. However, what is not known by many people is that there was a service tunnel under Skinner Street linking the two branches! These are now JD and Toni & Guy hairdressers, respectively. Debenhams have relocated after some year's absence from the town into an ultra-modern store on the Arc shopping complex.

Crescent House

Surveyors Lenny & Croft had offices here on Angel Hill during the 1840s. John Lenny had carried out an extensive survey of the town in 1822. John Croft went on to become Borough surveyor. During the 1920s, Sybil Andrews visited Cyril Power's studio in Crescent House. Heavily influenced by his art medium, lino cutting, both went on to become world-famous artists. The Crimean War cannon was removed to the Militia Barracks in Cemetery Road around 1864. Crescent House nowadays attracts estate agents.

Everards Hotel

Michael Everard, whose family had connections to the Suffolk Hotel, purchased the Woolpack Inn in 1864, renaming it Everards Hotel. It had a popular tap at the rear and a first-floor function room. Everards disappointingly closed in 1987. Only the façade was retained, and many architectural features, fireplaces and ancient carved beams disappeared. An archaeological dig at the rear found seventeen wells, part of a lost brewery when shops and offices were built. On the corner of Woolhall Street a wool hall indeed once stood.

Suffolk Hotel

Before 1833, this was a coaching inn on Buttermarket known as The Greyhound. Due to its antiquity, records go back before the sixteenth century and there are supposed to be tunnels to the abbey from its cellars! A tap at the rear, colloquially known as 'The Suffolk Shades', was extremely popular. The Suffolk, favourite watering hole of locals through the years, closed in 1996; it was split into two shops, and bunches of grapes on the pillars are the only indication of its former life.

Ridleys

This superlative grocery business run by the Ridley family at No. 36 Abbeygate Street started in 1801 in a building dating from around 1700. Thomas Ridley twice became mayor of the town in 1878 and 1882. In later years the business even went on to sell decorating materials next door! However, it was the wonderful evocative smells of cheeses, coffee beans and cured meats that met you as you crossed the threshold that many people can remember. Sadly, due to rising rates, it closed in 1996, replaced by Café Uno restaurant and then Prezzo.

J. W. Gibbs, Cornhill

William Gibbs was a pastry cook and confectioner on Cornhill from around 1855. His son Joseph took over and was still going in 1927 according to Pawseys directory of that year. Many years later it was the Bury Linen shop. In March 1965 a knocked-over paraffin stove set light to the shop, completely destroying it; the rebuilt shop is similar to its predecessor. It later became a branch of Croydon's jeweller's; Preston & Duckworth jeweller's then took it over.

Garrard's

This butcher's shop at No. 28 Abbeygate Street was one of two Garrard's in the town; the other was in Out Risbygate. W. H. Garrard was advertised as 'The Hygenic Butcher' and gained a reputation as a butcher's of high quality. Garrard's finished August 1985, taken over by the Dewhurst chain. Eventually this closed too and became Trotter & Deane in 1991. The shopfront was redesigned by Modece architects in 2012; managing director John Deane-Bowers was at the forefront of an upmarket clothiers.

Booty & Son

At the junction with Etna Road, Booty & Son, confectioners, dairy produce and greengrocers, survived after other shops were demolished in 1973 to make way for the link to the A14. Since the 1930s Booty's had delivered milk from the family farm at Timworth via a horse-drawn float, probably the last in the town. Its truism was 'the milk's yours, the bottle's ours'. After it closed it became a letting agent's. The giant silos of the Bury sugar factory are on the left.

The Bus Station & Odeon

In 1947, Brentgovel Street was a major route through the town when the Eastern Counties Omnibus Co. opened this station. In the background you can see the Art Deco Odeon cinema by Oscar Deutsch launched in 1937; it was renamed The Focus in 1975, sadly closing its doors in 1982. Demolition soon followed and this area was redeveloped, with a McDonald's on the station site, and a debatable shopping mall – Cornhill Walk – where once cinema goers flocked.

Northgate Station

Originally built as a terminus on the line from Ipswich, this station opened for use on Christmas Eve 1846. It was designed by the architect of Dublin station, Sancton Wood. When finished, it had a roof that projected out from the lead-capped twin towers; this roof was removed in 1893. The steam engine shown may be a 'Little Sharpie', manufactured for the Great Eastern Railway, 1867–72. The station and yards, once a major employer in the town, have seen the station's four lines reduced to two.

Lansbury House

Until its closure in 1903 this was the Three Tuns, one of only two public houses in Crown Street. It was later to become the headquarters of the local Labour Party, Lansbury House, from 1949 until 1997. George Lansbury was chairman of the National Labour Party during the 1930s. Always painted in the party's bright-red hues, since it became a private house the colours are more subdued. Adjacent, Tuns Lane is a reminder of the past connection to the property.

Raingate House, Raingate Street
This picture was taken soon after the house had been restored by the Town Trust in 1988.
The Trust grew out of an idea put forward during the architectural heritage year of 1975.
Left £87,000 by local benefactor Dr Alison Rae in 1988, the Trust buys buildings at risk and
renovates them, selling them on to enable the next project to be undertaken. Restored by
the Town Trust, plaques are then affixed to the properties.

Appleby Rose Garden, Abbey Gardens
John Tate Appleby was an American serviceman sent over to England in 1945 to teach celestial navigation to American flyers; he was not required as they were flying by day then. The highly educated Appleby enjoyed his sojourn so much he wrote a book called *A Suffolk Summer*, which is still in print. The royalties were left by him to help create and maintain this wonderful garden. There are various memorials to servicemen here, and today it is a place of tranquillity and contemplation.

Abbey Gardens

These beautiful gardens were opened in 1831 based on designs in Brussels. The creator and curator was Nathaniel Hodson. Then, there were subscriptions for entry varying from £2 to 6d! The Borough leased the gardens from 1912 from the owner, the Marquess of Bristol, eventually buying the freehold in 1953. A team of dedicated gardeners here has contributed to the town, winning numerous major floral awards over the years, and enabling visitors and residents to enjoy this outstanding amenity.

H. A. & D. Taylor

This company was once a major employer in the town and one of the top three East Anglian maltsters. It merged with Ipswich Maltings in 1957. The maltings in Out Northgate were put up for sale by H. C. Wolton in 1973 but did not attract any viable offers; demolition eventually followed. A branch of Kettering Tyres was then built and a national company, HiQ garage, is here now. Dating from 1846, The Railway Hotel on the right became The Linden Tree, around 1985.

Oast House

The last vestige of the Southgate brewery, which stood opposite on the corner of Maynewater Lane and Southgate Street, was this Oast House. Purchased by Edward Greene in 1868 on the death of owner, Henry Braddock, the brewery was demolished. It was in use for drying hops and malt through the rear of the White Hart (now Abbey Hotel) up to 1930, when it was known as the White Hart Maltings. In the 1980s, the building was converted into two apartments.

The Cattle Market

In 1852 a new cattle market entrance was opened off Risbygate Street. This livestock market enabled the firm of Henry Lacy Scott subsequently to operate a Wednesday auction of beasts that contributed to the town's standing. The latter part of the twentieth century saw these markets wane, resulting in this popular venue for residents and visitors alike being curtailed. A modern shopping centre, the Arc, was put forward, and shoppers' feet now tread where trotters and hooves once trod! The last vestige of the market, Pettit's tea hut, was gone by 2006.

The Settlers Hut

Often referred to as the Round House, this wooden hut has a very special place in the town's history. Built around 1864, it was used to settle accounts between buyers and sellers on market day at the cattle market; with this now gone a battle to try and save it started. Put into storage, Bury lost out mainly due to disinterest by the Arc developers; however, the Museum of East Anglian Life at Stowmarket stepped in, restored it and now displays it.

The Market Cross

A public building on the Cornhill has been here for hundreds of years in one shape or form. The elegant Market Cross dates from 1775/76 to designs by Robert Adam and wonderful stone carvings by local mason Thomas Singleton. The top floor, a theatre until 1819, became concert rooms with the opening of the Theatre Royal. In 1972 it became the town's art gallery and it was recently rebranded as Smiths Row. The ground floor had been used for municipal purposes for many years, leased now as a bookmaker's.

Former Borough Offices, Angel Hill

Sybil Andrews, famous local artist, created the heraldic cartouche on the 1937 pediment with the Borough motto 'shrine of a king, cradle of the law' in Latin for the Borough Arts & Craft architect, Basil Oliver. The rear 1966 Borough office extension has now been converted to apartments. The house to the left, now the Tourist Information Centre, was owned by eighteenth-century philanthropist Dr Poley Clopton; his bequest of an asylum (rest home) in the churchyard is now the Deanery.

Angel Hill

The Virginia creeper-covered Angel Hotel, built in 1775 on the site of three inns, dominates this open area. Charles Dickens stayed here and included the Angel in his first novel, *The Pickwick Papers*. A blue plaque testifies to this. Here the important Bury Fair was held from early medieval times until 1871, and was abolished by Parliament for being a nuisance. A popular annual Christmas Fayre rivalling its ancient forebear is now a major attraction. The 'Pillar of Salt' is a listed traffic sign from 1935!

The Athenaeum

In 1801 local banker James Oakes purchased this building at the southern end of Angel Hill. Francis Sandys, the architect of Ickworth Mansion, is thought to have carried out the refurbishment work. Oakes promptly sold off shares in the property to some fellow members of the thirty-seven-man corporation – hence Subscription Rooms. Over the years its Adam-style ballroom has played host to many important functions, but its observatory, installed after a lecture in 1859 by Sir George Airey, Astronomer Royal, is no longer used.

Elsey's Yard

Cyril Elsey of Westley Road had his builder's yard here in Risbygate Street. He was also a chairman of Bury Town FC for many years. When he died, this Grade II listed former seventeenth-century malthouse was on the building-at-risk register. Thanks to a £1.1 million heritage lottery grant, a complete restoration under the name 'The Malthouse Project' enabled provision for accommodation for St Matthews housing, a heritage centre and a café. It was completed in 2007.

Victoria Laundry, Victoria Street

This laundry started at No. 52 at the turn of the last century, when owned by John Palfrey and his initials are on the baskets. It then passed into the ownership of R. Haylock & Sons. There was competition from The Sanitary Laundry in Northgate Avenue and later from The Hand Laundry on the site of the old flax factory at Hardwick. The latter took over these two, with the Victoria eventually closing in the 1960s. Various businesses have been here since.

Northgate Street

This street, in antiquity known as High Street, led to the Northgate. This gate was demolished in the 1760s, along with the other four medieval town gates, to allow better access to the town. Horse-drawn traffic was very much the order of the day when this picture was taken, in marked contrast to the hustle and bustle of modern motor vehicles. Today, North Court Care home is where the flint wall was on the right.

Guildhall Street

A much used street scene of the Guildhall and possibly the oldest civic building in the country. Recent evidence uncovered details of how it has been serving the people of Bury St Edmunds from around the twelfth century as a meeting hall, court and council chamber. During the Second World War, the Royal Observer Corps had an ops room inside, which is still here; it may be the only one of its kind in the country. The Guildhall Project hopes to create a heritage centre here.

St Marys Square

The market place of the town eventually evolved into a fashionable place to live. The large house at the top of the picture was where the Maulkin family of maltsters lived. Fred King, who married Emily Maulkin in 1852, acquired it for his future St Edmunds brewery; it was later demolished before the First World War for Greene King's barley store. To the right are medieval houses and the grassed area has a wonderful terracotta planter of 1874 by Mark Blanchard, recently restored.

Chequer Square

This was an important open space in front of the religious entrance to the abbey. The house of John Baret, a wealthy fifteenth-century merchant, which was a forces study centre in the Second World War, is on the left almost facing Norman Tower House, which was once the Savings Bank. At the northern side of the Square, St Edmunds Masonic Lodge closed recently but originated from 1890 when the Six Bells, an important former coaching inn, finished. The obelisk moved in 1977 to create more parking and has the Borough coat of arms on, although it is almost obliterated now.

Whiting Street North

The flags and bunting were to celebrate the Coronation of George V in 1911. John Hollis Gill, photographer – his premises on the left at No. 77 – took this photograph! Once the Bricklayers Arms, the clapperboard-covered (uncommon to this area) Masons Arms has recently had an internal refurbishment. The shop of James Stockbridge on the corner sold confectionary; as much a magnet for children as when it was The Land of Green Ginger. It has been a wine bar under various guises for several years.

Mustow Street

Angel Hill used to be known as *le Mustowe*, The Muster – a place to gather. This name was carried down into this narrow street at the side of the abbey's precinct north wall. In 1926, despite much opposition, it was agreed to widen the road; the old timber-frame cottages, including the 200-year-old Star Inn (closed in 1923), were demolished. One small concession to the past was the reuse of ancient timbers in the rebuild of No. 17 Mustow Street.

Orchard Street and St John's Church

These houses, from 1866 onwards, were built on land that was indeed an orchard. Mortgages were given by the Bury St Edmunds Building Society providing the value of the property exceeded £110! St John's church, built in 1841/42 by architect William Ranger, became the much needed third parish church of the town, St John's infant's school soon following. The railings of the houses now add to the street scene, which has won several floral awards in recent years.

Buttermarket

The few changes here are in the buildings' usages. Cullen's outfitters have gone and so has the Suffolk Hotel (now shops). The Playhouse cinema on the right closed in 1959; its bucket seats went into the newly restored Theatre Royal. The much loved Playhouse became a Co-operative store, Quality House and it is now a branch of Argos. In the distance is the ever-constant Moyses Hall, the Borough Museum. One major difference today is the traffic management, as a rigid one-way system is in place.

Linden House

A keystone with 1813 BC inscribed is on an arch at the rear of this property, a clue to the owner. This was Salem Cottage, the home of Benjamin Cook. He was the father-in-law of successful grocer Thomas Ridley, who later lived here and added the three-storey frontage in 1880. Linden House was at No. 64 Cemetery Road until being renumbered and renamed No. 147 Kings Road in 1911. Owned by Anglian Water for many years, Pigeon Investments offices are now here.

Dairy Cottage, Home Farm Lane

This is now the only thatched property in Bury, following the great fire of 1608, when thatch was banned in the town centre. Built around 1837, this comprised two cottages when Ron Walton worked as dairyman in the 1950s and 1960s for Fulcher's Dairy of Whiting Street. Lionel Fulcher lived at Home Farm, once part of the Hardwick estate, owned by the Cullum family. When modern housing was built in the area, Dairy Cottage was used as a site office. Rather than being demolished it was renovated, receiving an award.

Ouida Memorial, Stamford Court

This drinking trough celebrates Victorian Bury-born author Louise De La Ramee, aka Ouida. It was erected to ardent pacifist Ouida (her childhood pronunciation of Louise) by *Daily Mirror* readers' subscriptions after her death in Italy in 1908. There are two bronze female figures, one of Courage holding a sword, the other Sympathy embracing a dog. Turned around when moved from its original position, it now looks forlorn; the junction where it now stands is no longer a quiet backwater.

War Memorial, Bury St. Edmunds.

War Memorial, Angel Hill

This was dedicated in October 1921 to the fallen from the First World War. The names of these 427 men are written in a book of remembrance that is kept in the cathedral, the pages of which are turned every day. The memorial is in the shape of a Celtic cross supposedly modelled on a long-lost cross in the abbey. Nowadays, wreaths to all conflicts are laid with all due reverence on Remembrance Sunday in November.

South African War Memorial, Cornhill

Known today as the Boer War, this island monument by celebrated sculptor A. G. Walker was unveiled by Lord Methuen on the auspicious date of 11 November 1904; it was surrounded by volleys of rifle fire by soldiers to the 193 men from all over Suffolk who died in the conflict. They had served in various regiments. Today, it is normally surrounded by parked cars and stalls on market days, but still looking no different from yesteryear.

The Martyrs Memorial

This Purbeck limestone obelisk was erected by public subscription in 1903 by local stonemason's Hanchets. Recorded on it are the details of seventeen Protestant martyrs who perished during the reign of Queen 'Bloody' Mary, 1553–58. Strangely none of the victims were from Bury but from such places as Hadleigh, Coddenham and Stoke by Nayland. They were ordinary folk such as weavers and labourers. It holds a prominent place in the churchyard, a fitting reminder to those brave souls.

87

Les Freeman

Flat cap, stockman's coat, kerchief and drooping woodbine were the trademarks of this feisty character, Les Freeman, the last rag-and-bone man in the town. After disposing of his 'goods' at Brahams or Barkers scrapyard, he went onto one of his haunts the Black Boy or The George in Out Westgate, as both had stabling for his horse. Sadly, he was found dead in an outhouse where he had lived the last few years of his life.

Chas Watson

Charles Watson & Co. had its origins in Bridewell Lane, adjacent to the Feoffment School. This site proved too small as a timber yard, so Watson's moved to larger premises in Southgate Street on former meadows known from the town's monastic days as Almoners Farm Barns. Watson's expanded, becoming builders' merchants, but were taken over by William Brown in 1982, and they in turn by Jewson's, who later moved to Moreton Hall. A housing estate was built by Redrow Homes on the large site.

Abbeygate Street Looking to Fire

This is one of several amazing photographs taken by W. S. Spanton, who had his photographic premises opposite this devastating fire of 1882. It had been set by failed tobacconist Simon Last, whose shop was near to the Hatter Street corner. The embers were still smouldering when Last's insurance claim went in! The results of all this were five years' hard labour for him, creation of the Borough Fire Brigade, and the building line set back.

Cupola House, Traverse

Thomas and Susan Macro owned an apothecary's here in 1693. The iconic Cupola overlooked a very different Cornhill, then a large open space. As the Victoria PH it was owned by the Jennings family during the late nineteenth century before Clarks Brewery purchased it, selling out to Greene King in 1917. In later years it fell into disrepair until a successful restoration in 2003. As Strada restaurant it suffered a disastrous fire in June 2012. It now awaits restoration to its former glory.

West Suffolk Hospital and St Peter's Church, Hospital Road
Formerly an ordnance depot from Napoleonic days, the Suffolk General Hospital, as it was known then, opened in January 1826. The purchase of land at Hardwick enabled a new hospital to be built in 1973; the old hospital was later cleared for new housing as Cornwallis/ St Peters Court. Intended for a chapel of ease for St Mary's, St Peter's was built in 1856 by renowned builder Thomas Farrow, who had carried out restoration on the Norman tower.

Nos. 32–33, Whiting Street

Part of the town's historic core, these two houses both had diverse pasts. On the left motor engineers T. H. Nice had their paint shop and service bay at the rear (now Finsbury Place), while on the right, where the bicycle is, was the Ten Bells pub. This was a beerhouse in Victorian times; after receiving a full licence it became the Duke of York following his visit to the town and it closed in 1910. Both are now residential.

Gibraltar Barracks, Newmarket Road

One of a few surviving examples in the country, these barracks were named after the Suffolks heroic defence of The Rock. It was built in 1878 to designs by Major Seddon R. E., the 12th Regiment of Foot, as the Suffolks (now part of Royal Anglian Regiment) were once known. Their greatest battle honour was victory over the French at the Battle of Minden, 1 August 1759, which is still celebrated today. The keep, housing the regimental museum and some curtain walls, is all that remains.

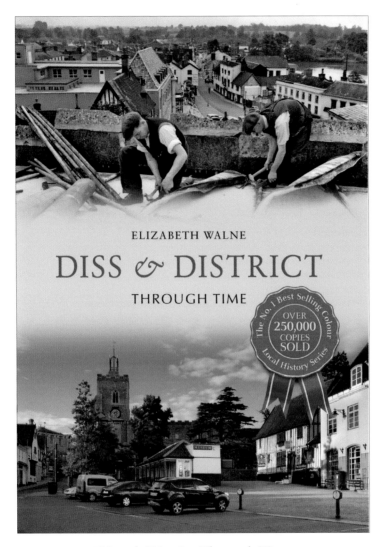

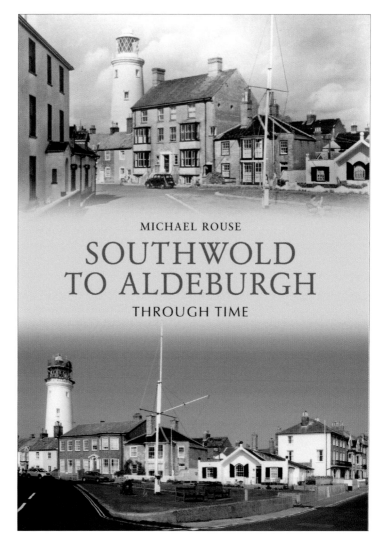

Southwold to Aldeburgh Through Time

Mike Rouse

This fascinating selection of photographs traces some of the many
ways in which the Suffolk coast from Southwold to Aldeburgh has
changed and developed over the last century.

978 1 4456 0772 6
96 pages, full colour